Extreme Training

for the

advanced

cellist

book one

by Cassia Harvey

CHP176

©2007 by C. Harvey Publications All Rights Reserved.

www.charveypublications.com - print books & free sheet music blog
www.learnstrings.com - PDF downloadable books & chamber music

Extreme Training for the Advanced Cellist
Book One
Cassia Harvey

©2006 C. Harvey Publications All Rights Reserved.

Extreme Training for the Advanced Cellist, Book One

Extreme Training for the Advanced Cellist, Book One 13

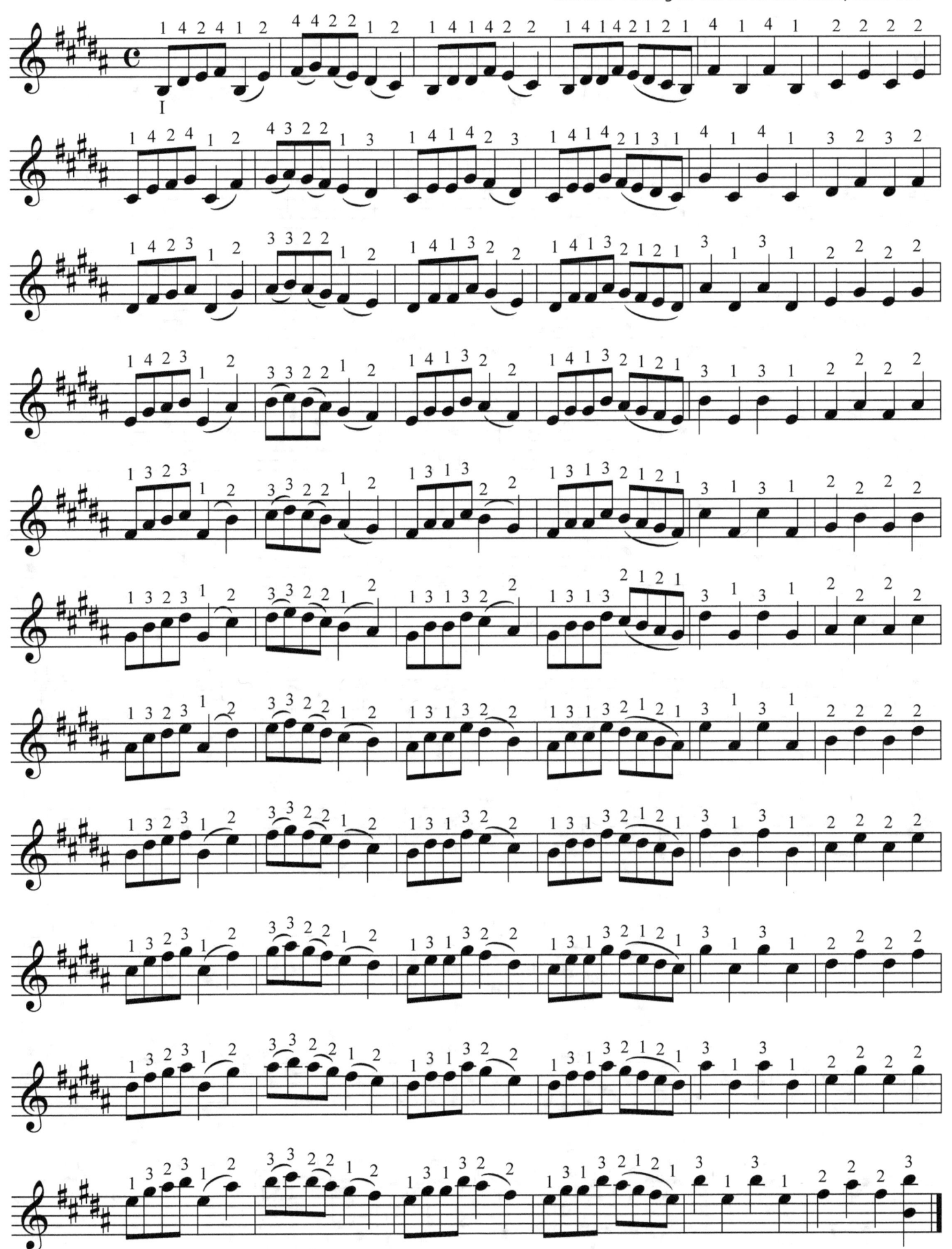

This entire page is played on the A string.

This entire page is played on the A string.

18 Extreme Training for the Advanced Cellist, Book One

©2006 C. Harvey Publications All Rights Reserved.

This entire page is played on the A string.

Extreme Training for the Advanced Cellist, Book One

This entire page is played on the A string.

26 Extreme Training for the Advanced Cellist, Book One

©2006 C. Harvey Publications All Rights Reserved.

This entire page is played on the A string.

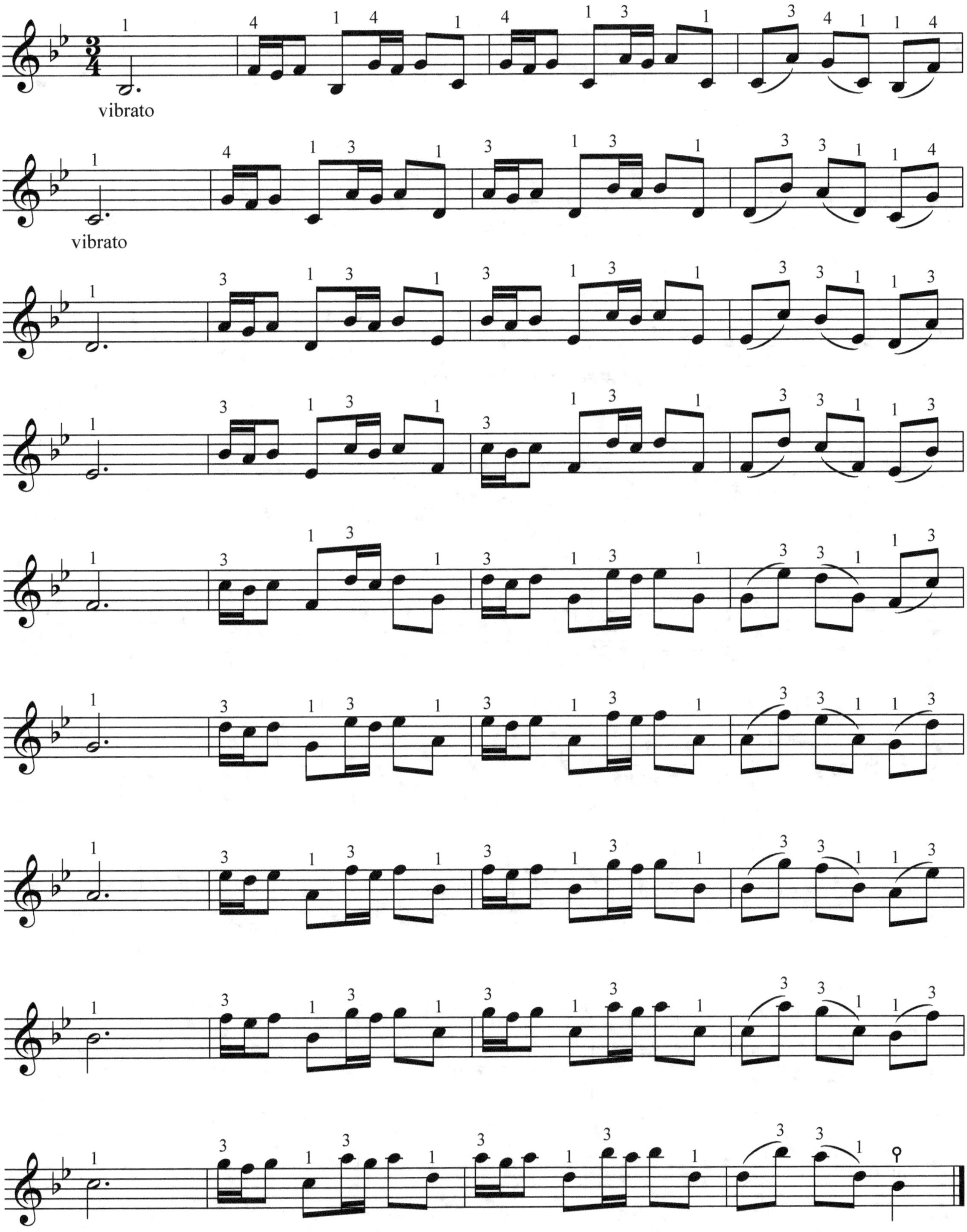
vibrato
vibrato

Extreme Training for the Advanced Cellist, Book One 31

©2006 C. Harvey Publications All Rights Reserved.

Extreme Training for the Advanced Cellist, Book One

34 Extreme Training for the Advanced Cellist, Book One

©2006 C. Harvey Publications All Rights Reserved.

Also available from www.charveypublications.com: CHP349
The Saint-Saens Cello Concerto No. 1 Study Book, Vol. 1

©2019 C. Harvey Publications All Rights Reserved.

www.ingramcontent.com/pod-product-compliance
Lightning Source LLC
Chambersburg PA
CBHW051427070526
44584CB00023B/3620